BROKEN PALACE
A COLLECTION OF POEMS, MICRO-TALES

ALIVA DUTTA

Copyright © Aliva Dutta
All Rights Reserved.

ISBN 978-1-63745-898-3

This book has been published with all efforts taken to make the material error-free after the consent of the author. However, the author and the publisher do not assume and hereby disclaim any liability to any party for any loss, damage, or disruption caused by errors or omissions, whether such errors or omissions result from negligence, accident, or any other cause.

While every effort has been made to avoid any mistake or omission, this publication is being sold on the condition and understanding that neither the author nor the publishers or printers would be liable in any manner to any person by reason of any mistake or omission in this publication or for any action taken or omitted to be taken or advice rendered or accepted on the basis of this work. For any defect in printing or binding the publishers will be liable only to replace the defective copy by another copy of this work then available.

DEDICATED TO MAA AND BABA

Contents

Preface — *vii*

Acknowledgements — *ix*

1. Hide — 1
2. Me Or You — 2
3. Who Are You? — 3
4. Unseen Cuts — 5
5. Country Life — 6
6. Mental Health Is Important — 8
7. 3 A.m — 10
8. Truth Or Lie ? — 12
9. Broken Palace — 14
10. Your Ruffled Hair — 16
11. Do You Feel The Same Way ? — 18
12. He-respect-she — 20
13. Flaws — 22
14. Confused — 23
15. Blend — 24
16. Contradiction — 25
17. Escape 2020 — 26
18. Pretend — 27
19. Forever — 28
20. Doubt — 29
21. Or — 30
22. Back Home — 31

Contents

23. Did You Find Your Home?	32
24. Your Listener	33
25. Broken Souls Treat Others A Little Well	35
26. Smokes And Bottles	37
27. Spring	39
28. Little Things That Matter	40
29. Is It So Difficult ?	41
30. Over And Over	42
31. The End	43
About The Author	45

Preface

Writing has always been a great support , healer to me .Although I am good at expressing my emotions and feelings verbally but over the last four years I discovered that not all emotions and feelings can be expressed verbally ,that is when I started writing almost every other day.Slowly and gradually it became a part of daily life.Being an avid reader since childhood , the secret desire to have collection of own poems always lingered somewhere at the back of my mind.

I started writing while I was in school but the habit of constant writing developed from 2016 .And the poems in this book are some of my favourite ones over the years .

2020 ,indeed was a tough year for all of us with our own battles but we all are sailing strong through it. Some poems in the book were the feelings that I came across in 2020 and I know most of you (The one reading it) have gone through the same. And few poems are on social issues that we face at some point of life. In the book most poems are emotions that I actually felt and some are the fragments of my imagination.

I hope you feel connected to my poems while reading this book.

Thank You for picking up my book or rather I would say - Thank You for reading my unexpressed emotions.

Happy Reading
ALIVA DUTTA

Acknowledgements

First and foremost ,I would like to thank my parents for making me believe in own self and encouraging me to write since my childhood.My family members also supported me greatly ,they also deserves a great thank you.

Secondly ,I would like to thank my teachers from St.Joseph's Convent Higher Secondary School, Tezpur, Assam who always encouraged me to read good books and guided me thoroughly.Also great thanks to all my teachers of Assam Agricultural University for all the encouragement and support.And thanks to all the teachers who taught,inspired in different phases.

Always thankful to all my friends of school, junior college, university who helped me and read my writings throughout the years.Thanks to my dearest seniors and lovely juniors who infused in me lots of positivity.

A huge thanks to all my friends I met through NSS , probably the best people in my life.

Thanks to all the people I came across in different times of my life who shared with me their story ,thus many became an inspiration for me to write.

I would like to thank God for blessing me .

1. HIDE

Perfectly encysted with lavender flowers
It's kept in a corner of my heart
This time I won't let anyone know
About You
This time I won't let anyone know
About that pure feeling.
Because , they will simply destroy it
With all their
Not so required point of views
Probably, even you won't know about it
Because it's kept safely now,
Perfectly encysted with lavender flowers.

2. ME OR YOU

Intertwined emotions,
In the sea of known and unknown feelings.
Complicated souls
Trying to act simple .
But the inner soul, heart
Tired.
Happiness
A not-so-big deal feeling for few,
Once in a lifetime feeling for many.
Same with sadness...
We are just a complicated generation
Mostly trying to figure out
What exactly it feels
And what do we need from life.
Is it bundles of love or truckloads of success,
Yet we fail to form the bridge between the two.
Complicated, over-stressed generation
Needs food for soul more now...

3. WHO ARE YOU?

Who are you?
A tiny dot
In the huge galaxy,
A collection of atoms
In the huge earth,
A lost soul
Finding home,
A dust of particle
In huge surrounding.
Who are you?
An accumulation of emotions
In this hyper practical World,
A silent voice
In this huge over noisy earth,
An individual
Finding yourself.
What defines us exactly?
Maybe nothing
Maybe everything.
We will all return back to the soil
At the end ,
Or maybe only our bodies will perish
Our soul might home again,

In another lost soul..
WHO ARE WE?
WHO ARE YOU?
WHO AM I?

4. UNSEEN CUTS

Cuts with no wounds and scars
Only with dried up tears.
Ohh! You can't explain
How it feels?
But I understand
How badly it hurts?
Right in the middle of the night,
When you lay awake
In that darkness
Engulfs you..
Cuts with no wounds and scars,
Hurts directly to your heart.

5. COUNTRY LIFE

Sometimes you get addicted
To the silence.
The calmness only
Country life can offer you.
A little less humans surrounding you
And a lot more of green rice fields, magnificent sky
Full of thousands of stars,
A bench made of bamboo,
Huge ponds full of uncountable fish,
And you sit there silently,
Closing yours eyes.
Those are the moments
You will realize ,
Materialistic happiness is so superficial
You life, your soul
Needs love, care, nurture
That only nature, silence can offer .
Most importantly you can offer yourself
Not materials..
And how much important it is to move back to roots,
Those rice fields, huge tea gardens, ponds..
Your land is calling you...
Your home is calling you..

It's time,
It's time my friend,
To return back to your roots.

6. MENTAL HEALTH IS IMPORTANT

Do you believe in fairytales?
Where everything has a happy ending?
Where it's all about positive winning over negative..
Probably no ,
We don't believe in those anymore.
Our demons have taken over our angels now,
Our anxiety, depression, stress, inner negativity has taken over our sweet innocence.
We are getting insane with each passing day..
We all are,
Dealing with it with our own devices and magic,
Few believing in miracles,
Few taking medication and professional help,
Few just letting understand, what exactly is happening,
Few just being wandering nomads in this huge crowd....
Ohh!!! I am not here to preach you
Just to let you know
"Let's atleast hope for happy endings
Let's atleast believe in our fairy-tales"
Cheers to the ones who are in this battle alone
Trying to fix everything own self.
Superheros (No one says you that right, but you are)

Hope you find peace in all these mess.
YOU ARE MORE POWERFUL THAN YOUR IMAGINATION.

7. 3 A.M

Creeping into your bedroom, through the ventilators.
The sound of fan
Reaching your ears.
And it's all dark,
You are sweating profusely
You can't breathe properly.
And try to move out of your bed
Searching for the glass of water
That will be somewhere on your bedside table.
You find yourself in tears
And you even don't know what happened..
You sit there and wonder
"Are you actually fine and content with life? "
You grab your phone
Type a text but never send.
You try to hold yourself back
Put on your playlist and try to sleep
It's 3 AM
But you find yourself in tears
And unknowingly you sleep.
That's how you grow up
Holding yourself back
Being independent

In true sense
Is being with own self when no one is there.

8. TRUTH OR LIE ?

The Poets,
The Writers,
They lie...
How easily they beautify
A feeling,
How easily they make
Us feel
Things are getting well,
How easily they make us
Know about their emotions.
But maybe
They lie too.
Elaborate the goodness
And diminish the evil.
But, we all know
How is reality.
The bright sunflower get pale too,
The elegant rose dries too,
The rain is not about love always
It breaks dreams too,
Floods away everything sometimes.
The Mountains are full of rocks too
Your leg shall hurt.

But the poets only glorify the
Beauty.
And writes poetry
To manifest how strong they are,
Enduring all pain.
The Poets
The Authors
They Lie...

9. BROKEN PALACE

My palace is broken now
Shattered ,
The glittering lights
Are gone,
It's all dim now.
But, I have loved this
Broken palace now.
Atleast it doesn't hold
Promises which were fake,
Moments that were momentary,
And people who just
Required your presence
In gloomy days,
To talk about their broken heart.
And completely forgot,
When you needed them.
Grown in love with the darkness
And silence .
In my broken palace,
Ohh!! No
You won't get a invitation in my broken palace,
Because, I might not have the courage to deal with
Another ray of hope,

That gets black soon.
Before I realize.

10. YOUR RUFFLED HAIR

All the times
My heart aches
All the times
I feel a different pain engulfing me
I remember you.
I know I shouldn't,
I know you are long gone,
And lost and probably we won't meet ever.
But that smiling face,
The ruffled hair,
That eyes full of broken dreams
And I don't know if that was ,,,,
"Love"
The ever fancy word people or my favourite writers say.
I just know
I want to meet you
Just once more.
And listen to your untold stories,
And cry my heart out .
Ohh!! I don't know if it was love,
I just know after that I could not feel that way
For anyone who crossed my path after you

I was devoid of emotions.
All the feelings I felt before You and after You
Doesn't hold true now.
All the poetry I wrote for someone else
Seems fake to me now.
You were the magic that made me
A stronger and better person.
Ohh! I didn't nor will I cry for you
Because those memories are something I will hold on
Forever and ever..

11. DO YOU FEEL THE SAME WAY ?

When the heart yearns
When it can't hold anymore
And you find yourself all alone.
Dozens of people become meaningless
Because you are too petrified
To share your feelings.
And for long and long
You kept it within you
It hurts right, it breaks you down
It weakens you.
You are amidst a huge crowd
But you know you can't share your
That part of pain with anyone
And it builds and builds inside you.
The world is too cruel .
And you get the feeling,
"Maybe I am too bad,
I could never find the answer.
All I know is that
I wish I could share
I wish I could trust
Because it definitely breaks down.

Maybe it will all be washed away
With the ashes of my pyre
When I will be gone forever
I wish I could run away
This pain is immensely painful.
Even if I share
It definitely doesn't and won't lessen my amount of pain."

12. HE-RESPECT-SHE

There are
Thousands of words
We all want to share.
Thousands of emotions
We all want to express.
But then
The society will judge.
Starting from the days
Of early teens
Talking about
How we shouldn't consider
Menstruation as a taboo
And follow the age old superstitions.
To early 20's
Talking about
How we deserve nights
Walks
That are safe enough
To walk
That are safe enough
To be alone.
We just speak and speak
No one much bothers

To listen.
Few things
Every normal woman goes through,
You don't need to be a feminist .
(Though you will be called one, all the times you speak up)
Why to blame the Men?
Witnessed Woman who wishes to
Hold back the age old taboos more,
Who never teaches their sons
To respect Woman,
Maybe Maybe
The next generations won't be like this.
(All we can hope)
Maybe the Men and Women
Of my generation,
Will teach their sons to respect Women.
Will teach their daughters to speak up
And not compromise.
The World will be a better place
When HE and SHE respects both
And achieves milestones together.

13. FLAWS

Fix the broken golden crown with the golden threads,
Because flaws are not accepted anymore
The more your flaws get exposed the more you become vulnerable.
And vulnerable species doesn't sustain for long.

14. CONFUSED

In between so many love stories and one sided love,
There exists a kind of story without a starting or ending.
It just happened with the flow, inspired you and then went away from life
Neither you can wait for closure because it didn't start,
Nor you can let it go because it didn't end,
You will forever remain in a state of confusion.

15. BLEND

I love the way we all are composed of, a little evil mixed with goodness.

I love people who are grey, a perfect mixture of black and white.

After all too much of white is too dull.

And people who pretend to be complete white are the worst of it kind.

Always remember, no human being can be composed of only goodness.

I love the way the way I am composed of,

A little evil mixed with goodness.

16. CONTRADICTION

If it was full of colour for her,it was monochrome for him .
If she was a metaphor, he was a plain phrase
She beholden emotions and he was full of reality.
The two contradictions tried to find the meeting point,
Where their desires and dreams would intersect.
Wandering around in the pool of emotions and reality
They believed that one fine day they will make life worth living for.

17. ESCAPE 2020

Didn't you just become the perfect escape for me ?
Away from my failures
Away from my confused feeling
Away from my wrong decisions
Mostly away from people...
You did become a perfect escape.
Even though I will hate 2020 for numerous reasons,
I will always cherish 2020 for giving me the perfect escape.
The less of human being and the more of knowing own self,
Was probably the perfect escape we all waited for.

18. PRETEND

DO YOU HATE...
The person who made you realize what love feels like
Or
The person whom you could never express you feelings
Or
The best friend whom you loved the most ,who left you when you needed them the most,
Or
The person who showed you dreams but broke your heart
Or
That friend who betrayed you in the best possible way...
The answer is NO
You can never hate the one
Whom you loved once a lot.
Even after years
The soft corner stays for them
Sometimes,I feel we all pretend to hate them
To deceive ourselves.

19. FOREVER

She wore the perfect shade of pink,
He wore the perfect shade of blue.
She had her pearl necklace,
He had his coloured tie.
But they weren't holding hands today,
Because they were placed in their coffins .
But shall be placed together
Forever and ever,
With each other but can't hold each other.
A virus took away their life,
Or making them rest in peace forever.

20. DOUBT

And I still wonder
What hurts me more
Your ignorance,
Or your honesty.
Your unspoken words,
Or your truth.

21. OR

Should one hold on to something that never belonged to them
But is precious to their heart??
OR
Should one let it go and hold on to something
That might belong to them if they want to ?

22. BACK HOME

I was lost in the woods
The path was full of gravels,
The elevation of the land was high,
And I was just wandering around
Finding the way out..
And then my eyes witnessed the bright light coming from a specific direction..
It was glazing brightness,
The light penetrated the dense woods and reached me..
I traced the light for long,
Found my path .
And I was back home ..
When you are lost in life just follow your inner light...
Ask ownself "What exactly is the reason for your existence? "
The answers your heart gives you will definitely be your guiding light..
YOU WILL BE BACK HOME..

23. DID YOU FIND YOUR HOME?

At the end of the day we just need a home,
Someone who makes you feel home,
Dozens of people in your life ,
Hundreds of words exchanged everyday,
But you are still a nomad,
Maybe your home is searching you or vice-versa ,
And once the home is broken it takes lots of trust and patience to rebuild it,
Maybe the person who makes you feel home is yet to enter your life.
Till then make your heart and soul your little small home...

24. YOUR LISTENER

Shall be listening
To your dreams, long lost hobbies
About the poetry you loved in your 10th Standard
Or, about the person who broke your heart in 12th Grade.
Never ever, shall I be someone
Who will make fun of your future plans,
They might seem unrealistic to the World
But, I shall only encourage you,
At Least with words and huge positive energy.
Never shall you feel negative vibes from me
When you share your ideas.
But! But !But!
Please don't ask me
About mine,
I shall talk about all the things I messed up in life,
I don't know to see the little good in me,
I don't have any positively for myself,
Don't ask me about my dreams,
You will get all negative vibes..
I am a positive person when you share your story
But a huge negative person when it's about me.
I never could look myself as anything worth,
I shall always be useless in my eyes..

But, trust me
You shall never regret to share your part of story with me,
I can be a great listener.
The few who knew it stayed back in my life

25. BROKEN SOULS TREAT OTHERS A LITTLE WELL

People who show you
That the world is not
A lovely place,
People who makes you
Feel that you are just miserable,
People who makes
Your tear glands active,
People who gives that feeling
That your heart will rip apart,
Are the best kind of people in your life.
You can grow well
Only if the thorns prick you.
You will know how actual care and love feels like,
Only if the one you loved the most
Ripped that part of you,
Which carried lots of love and emotions.
Your confidence needs to be broken
Multiple times
For you to believe in yourself.
All the times it broke a part of you

BROKEN PALACE

Were the times you became a little stronger.
Little by little the kid in you
Will know
How the actual world feels like..
The ones who never experienced how
Precious pain can feel
Are the ones who can never think once
Before breaking you apart again.
A broken soul
Always treats others a little well
Always.

26. SMOKES AND BOTTLES

Shredded,
The deliberate pieces
With lots of care.
Because you know
It shall hurt .
The toxic content of those pieces
Is exceptionally high,
The red alert .
You had to use,
The best techniques ,
To tear them apart from you.
Aren't we all attracted a little more
To toxicity?
Whether it's toxic material,
Or toxic people
That breaks your soul.
The half finished cigarette
Needs to be thrown away now,
Because you have done
Enough damage.
The old bottle of red wine,
Needs to be given away.

Your health needs
As much as love,
As the person who left you.
That aura needs to be forgotten
You deserve all the love.

27. SPRING

The dreams were left buried ..
The dreams got washed away with the first rain of monsoon..
The dreams got dried with the first sunny day of summer ..
The dreams got frozen with the first snowfall of winter..
But then came spring,
With open arms it taught to dream again..
With its freshness it said " Spread happiness through your dreams "

28. LITTLE THINGS THAT MATTER

Meet new people .
Read books by unknown and infamous authors.
Fall in deep love with someone's words.
Dance with the beats of raindrops .
Sing louder under the open sky .
Plant saplings, see them grow bit by bit .
Talk with people who inspire you .
And don't hesitate to start a conversation .
Help the poor roadside beggar, if possible buy him a meal.
Live life to the fullest and on your own terms.
Remember to make your parents proud because someone back home is waiting for your success

29. IS IT SO DIFFICULT ?

Why is it so difficult for us
To appreciate people,
To let them know
They matter to us.
Why is it so easy for us
To cry when they are gone,
And speak about their greatness,
When they can't even hear it.
When they are gone so far,
That our voice won't even reach them.
You and Me...
We all have truckloads of sins,mistakes,guilt
We are all same.

30. OVER AND OVER

Over and over...
The heart knows the consequences,
Still prefers to jump in the grave.
The grave holds the pain and hopes...
They say "Pain Demands to be Felt"
And the heart just follows it.
Whom shall the heart trust,
In this world of grave and graveyards.
The soul feels tourmented at times,
But still pushes the mind and body.
After all,the soul is the element
That has seen multiple births and rebirths
The soul believes that ,
"Things will fall in place eventually"
And one fine day,
The sun will be a little more brighter
And you will learn to dream again.

31. THE END

And tomorrow
If I lay on the deathbed.
Come with a bunch of purple flowers,
Might be an aristocratic orchid
Or an unwanted weed,
For I want the last goodbye
Wrapped in the colour
Which is close to my heart.
And tomorrow
If I lay on the deathbed.
Recite my favourite poems
In my funeral
For I want the last bye
With words from my cherished poets.

About The Author

Aliva Dutta , born and brought up in one of the most calm and clean place of Assam,Tezpur .She originally belongs to a small town called Rangapara .She attended her schooling in St.Joseph's Convent Higher Secondary School,Tezpur ; most of her reading and writing habits developed in school and definitely because of the wonderful and encouraging teachers of Convent school. She did her 12th from Pragjyotika Junior College,Titabar,Jorhat in Science Stream and her Bsc (Agriculture) from Assam Agricultural University(AAU) ,Jorhat,Assasm. The course of 4 years in AAU completely changed her life by giving her oppurtunities to represent university/state in both National and International level. She is currently pursuing her Masters from Banaras Hindu University .

She is also an avid reader and also a book-reviewer .ORDER-IN-A-MESS ,is her Instagram account where she posts book reviews . Her poems are inspired from human emotions and nature .

Apart from that she is interested in debating and Model United Nations(MUN),infact all forms of public speaking.She participated in both State level and National level debates , was also the Debating and Study Cirlcle Secretary in her college.She and her friends also started the AAU-MUN in Assam Agricultural University. Last but not the least,she is a trained Bharatanatyam Dancer and dance adds happiness and calmness to her life.

www.ingramcontent.com/pod-product-compliance
Lightning Source LLC
LaVergne TN
LVHW041547060526
838200LV00037B/1176